Stories from Faiths

HINDUISM

Anita Ganeri

www.heinemannlibrary.co.uk
Visit our website to find out more
information about Heinemann
Library books.

To order:
☎ Phone +44 (0) 1865 888066
▤ Fax +44 (0) 1865 314091
▦ Visit www.heinemannlibrary.co.uk

Heinemann Library is an imprint of Capstone Global Library Limited, a
company incorporated in England and Wales having its registered office
at 7 Pilgrim Street, London, EC4V 6LB – Registered company number:
6695582

"Heinemann" is a registered trademark of Pearson Education Limited,
under licence to Capstone Global Library Limited

Editor: Anand Mani
Designer: Harleen Mehta, Tarang Sagar
Picture Researchers: Dimple Bhorwal, Himanshu Chaudhary, S Kripa
Art Director: Rahul Dhiman
Client Service Manager: Aparna Malhotra
Project Manager: Smita Mehta
Lineart: Sibi N Devasia
Colouring Artists: Subhash Vohra, Danish Zaidi, Ashish Tanwar
Originated by Chroma Graphics (Overseas) Pte Ltd
Printed and bound in China by CTPS

ISBN 978-0-431-08222-6 (hardback)
13 12 11 10 09
10 9 8 7 6 5 4 3 2 1

ISBN 978-0-431-08229-5 (paperback)
14 13 12 11 10
10 9 8 7 6 5 4 3 2 1

British Library Cataloguing in Publication Data
Ganeri, Anita, 1961–
  Hinduism. – (Stories from faiths)
  294.5
A full catalogue record for this book is available from the British
Library.

Acknowledgements

We would like to thank the following for permission to reproduce
photographs (t = top, b = bottom, c = centre, l = left, r = right, m =
middle): Stelian Ion/ Shutterstock: 4t, K Ananthan/ The Hindu images:
5, K Gopinathan/ The Hindu images: 7b, Q2A Media Picture Bank/
Tarang Saggar: 8t, G R N Somashekar/ Business Line/ The Hindu
images: 10t, Ritu Raj Konwar/ The Hindu images: 13t, Sunil Lal/
Dreamstime: 14t, A M Faruqui/ The Hindu images: 16t, Bhakti Vedanta
Trust: 19t, A M Faruqui/ The Hindu images: 20t, Q2A Media Picture
Bank/ Tarang Saggar: 23t, S S Kumar/ The Hindu images: 24b, Avrajyoti
Mitra/ Flickr: 27b, India Picture: 28t.

Q2AMedia Art Bank: 6, 7, 9, 10, 11, 12-13, 15, 17, 18, 21, 22, 25, 26–27,
29.

Cover photograph of a girl decorating a float for Diwali in Reunion
reproduced with permission of Chris Hellier/ Corbis.

We would like to thank Q2AMEDIA for invaluable help in the preparation
of this book.

Every effort has been made to contact copyright holders of material
reproduced in this book. Any omissions will be rectified in subsequent
printings if notice is given to the publishers.

Disclaimer

All the Internet addresses (URLs) given in this book were valid at
the time of going to press. However, due to the dynamic nature of
the Internet, some addresses may have changed, or sites may have
changed or ceased to exist since publication. While the author and
publishers regret any inconvenience this may cause readers, no
responsibility for any such changes can be accepted by either the
author or the publishers.

Contents

Some words are printed in bold, **like this**. You can find out what they mean in the glossary.

What is Hinduism?

Hinduism is one of the world's oldest religions, dating back at least 4,500 years. Hindus themselves prefer to call their religion **sanatana dharma**, or "eternal teaching". For them, Hinduism does not simply mean a set of religious beliefs and rules to be followed. It is seen as a way of living, guiding people in everything they do. Today, most of the world's 1,000 million Hindus still live in India where Hinduism began. Others have settled in countries such as Britain, Canada and the USA.

Beliefs and worship

Hindus believe in an eternal spirit, called **Brahman**, an invisible force beyond the world in which we live. Some Hindus called Brahman "God". Hindus may worship Brahman in the form of **deities** (gods and goddesses) who represent Brahman's different powers and qualities. Hindus believe that every living thing has a soul. When you die, your soul is reborn in another body. This happens again and again until, by living a good life, you break free of the cycle and reach **moksha** (liberation).

Hindu stories

In Hinduism, stories play an important part. They have been told for centuries to teach people about their faith in a way that is easy to understand. Hindu children hear these stories from an early age. Later they read them in books and comics or watch them on the television. Stories about the lives and adventures of the gods and goddesses are very popular. These come from the Hindu sacred texts. You can read some of these stories in this book.

Children learn about gods and goddesses through the stories that they are told.

Rama Rescues Sita

The ancient kingdom of Kosala in India was once ruled by King Dasaratha. He was a wise and generous ruler, greatly loved by everyone. The king had four sons – Rama, Bharata, Lakshmana and Satrughna. Prince Rama was the eldest and his father's pride and joy.

King Dasaratha was getting old and he wanted Rama to be the next king. News spread quickly around the kingdom, and a grand **coronation** was arranged in the capital city of Ayodhya. But not everyone was happy. Rama's stepmother, Queen Kaikeyi, wanted her son, Bharata, to be king instead. She went to see King Dasaratha.

Rama left Ayodhya with his wife, Sita, and his brother, Lakshmana.

The Ramayana

The story of Rama comes from the **Ramayana**, one of the most popular Hindu sacred texts. The Ramayana is a poem with 24,000 verses, arranged into seven books. It is thought to have been composed some 4,000 years ago by a wise man called Valmiki. However, it was not written down until much later.

"Long ago, I saved your life on the battlefield," she told the king. "And you granted me two wishes in return. My first wish is for Bharata to be king, instead of Rama. And my second wish is for Rama to be sent to live in the forests for 14 years."

The king begged the queen to have pity but she would not change her mind. So later that day, Rama left the palace behind and set off for the forest with his wife, Sita, and his brother, Lakshmana.

Many years went by. Rama, Sita and Lakshmana lived in a cottage in the forest.

One day, Rama and Lakshmana went out hunting to catch a beautiful golden deer that Sita wanted to keep as a pet. While they were gone, an old man came to the door dressed as a holy man.

But this was no ordinary stranger.

▼ A priest reads the Ramayana in a **mandir**, or temple.

▲ These are images of Rama and Sita in a Hindu mandir.

Lord Rama

The hero of the Ramayana, Prince Rama, is worshipped by many Hindus as a god. In Hindu belief, Lord Vishnu visited the earth in different forms at times of great danger. These forms are known as the **avatars** of Vishnu. Rama was the seventh avatar. Hindus regard Rama as an ideal being, as a son, husband, father, king and human being.

This was Ravana, the terrible ten-headed demon king, in disguise. He dragged Sita to his chariot and flew back to his kingdom, Lanka.

When Rama and Lakshmana returned, they found the cottage empty. Sita was gone. They searched everywhere, but Sita was nowhere to be found.

Rama was filled with grief. In despair, he went to see Sugriva, lord of the monkeys, to ask for his help. Sugriva showed him a shining jewel.

"Four days ago, I saw Ravana riding through the sky with Sita. As they flew over us, she dropped this," he said, handing Rama the jewel.

"That is Sita's jewel – it must have been her," cried Rama. "And with your help, we will find her."

Sugriva gathered a huge army of monkeys and bears. Together, they set off to search for Sita.

After many days of travelling, Rama and his army of bears and monkeys reached the southernmost tip of India. But the island of Lanka, where Sita was imprisoned, lay many miles away across the sea. How were they going to reach it? The monkeys turned to their general, Hanuman, the wise and fearless son of the god of the wind.

With a single, gigantic leap, Hanuman jumped right across the ocean to Lanka. Then he shrank to the size of a cat and crept into Ravana's palace. There he found Sita, being kept prisoner in a grove of trees.

"Do not be afraid, my lady," said Hanuman. "As soon as I get back, Rama will lead his army to Lanka to rescue you."

Hanuman leapt back across the sea and gave Rama the good news. Rama was overjoyed.

When Rama and Lakshmana were out hunting, the demon king, Ravana, dragged Sita away to Lanka.

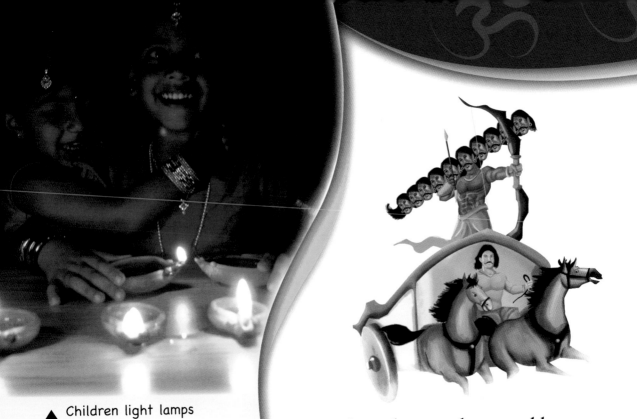

▲ Children light lamps to celebrate Diwali.

Diwali Festival

Rama and Sita's triumphant return to Ayodhya is remembered in October or November when Hindus all over the world celebrate the festival of Diwali. On Diwali night, people decorate their homes and temples with small oil lamps, called **diyas**. The lamps are lit to guide Rama and Sita safely home. Sweets are prepared at home and exchanged with relatives and friends. Children have fun lighting firecrackers.

Together, the monkeys and bears built a great bridge of rocks and trees across the sea. Then Rama marched his huge army across to Lanka.

Ravana's spies had warned him that Rama was coming. Furious, Ravana summoned his generals and demon soldiers together.

"Let the battle begin!" he shrieked.

As the fighting raged, Ravana's army was quickly defeated. With most of his army destroyed, it was Ravana's turn to face Rama.

With a blood-curdling cry, Ravana rode into battle in his golden war chariot, pulled by eight horses. As the sky grew darker, Ravana and Rama circled each other, waiting for the other to make the first move. Suddenly, Ravana picked up a javelin and hurled it at Rama. Rama was ready and smashed it with a javelin of his own.

Then Rama took an arrow made by the gods. This arrow never missed its target. Rama fired it at Ravana. It hit the demon king straight in the heart and he fell to the ground, dead.

Reunited, Rama, Sita and Lakshmana returned to Ayodhya. There, Rama and Sita were crowned king and queen.

In the battle, Rama finally killed Ravana.

Holika, the Wicked Witch

There was once a demon king called Hiranyakashipu who believed that he was God. Woe betide anyone who did not bow down and worship him when he entered the room.

King Hiranyakashipu had a son called Prahlad. Prahlad was gentle and kind and loved by all. Like everyone else in the palace, Prahlad believed that his father was God.

King Hiranyakashipu expected everyone to do what he wanted. Anyone who disobeyed was punished.

One day, Prahlad was playing near a potter's house in the village when he saw the potter praying.

"What are you doing?" he asked.

"I am praying to Lord Vishnu, who is God," replied the potter, "to save the life of my kittens. They fell into a pot and were put in the **kiln** by mistake."

"You should be praying to my father," Prahlad said.

"Why should I pray to your father?" said the potter, in surprise. "Your father isn't God."

▲ Children rub coloured powder on each other to celebrate Holi.

Holi Festival

The story of Prahlad, the king's son, is remembered in February or March when Hindus celebrate the festival of Holi. At this time people spray each other with coloured paints and powders. This also reminds Hindus of the story of how the mischief-loving god, Krishna, once drenched his friends, the milkmaids, with coloured water.

▲ Sweets are a very important part of any Hindu festival.

Festival Food

At Holi and other Hindu festivals, people visit their friends and relations with gifts of sweets. The sweets are mostly made from milk, nuts and sugar. People make the sweets at home or buy them from sweet shops.

Prahlad looked nervous. He hoped that the king did not get to hear what the potter had said or the potter would be killed.

But then the potter lifted the pot out of the kiln and Prahlad heard little squeaking sounds. It was the potter's kittens, all perfectly safe and well!

From that day on, Prahlad no longer believed that his father was God. Like the potter, he worshipped Lord Vishnu.

Some time later, the king summoned Prahlad to him.

"Who is the greatest being in the universe?" he asked him.

"You are the king, Father," said Prahlad, carefully. "But Lord Vishnu is God. And God is greater than anyone."

The king tried to convince Prahlad that he was wrong. He told him that he was the most powerful being on earth and that nothing could kill him.

"I agree with what you say father," he calmly replied. "But that does not make you God."

The king was furious. His face turned dark with rage.

"Take this foolish boy away," he bellowed at his soldiers, "and throw him into a pit of poisonous snakes."

The soldiers threw Prahlad into a pit of snakes. But none of the snakes would bite him, for Lord Vishnu was keeping him safe.

By now, the king was in a terrible temper. That night, when Prahlad was fast asleep, the king sent the royal elephants to trample him. But again, Lord Vishnu protected Prahlad and the elephants stopped and bowed meekly in front of him. Prahlad did not even wake up.

The snakes coiled around Prahlad and let him stroke their heads.

▲ Every year, on the night before Holi, people burn images of Holika.

Burning of Holika

Holi gets its name from Holika, the wicked witch. It is celebrated as a victory of good over evil. To remember the events of the story, people light bonfires and burn images of Holika. They also throw offerings of coconuts and rice into the fire to say thank you to Agni, the god of fire.

The soldiers dragged Prahlad back to the king.

"You've had a very lucky escape," the king spluttered.

"It wasn't luck, father," replied Prahlad. "God was looking after me."

At this, King Hiranyakashipu almost exploded with rage. He went to see his sister, a wicked witch called Holika.

Holika had a special magical power that had been given to her by the gods. She could pass through a fire without getting harmed by the flames.

When King Hiranyakashipu told her what had happened, she came up with an evil plan.

"We'll build a giant bonfire," cackled Holika, "and I'll carry Prahlad into the flames. My magical powers will protect me from the fire but Prahlad will not have this protection. This way we can get rid of Prahlad for ever."

Hiranyakashipu immediately agreed to the plan. Next day, a huge pile of wood was laid in the courtyard. Holika climbed on top of the pile with Prahlad. She sat in the middle and then placed Prahlad in her lap.

"Don't be frightened," she told him. "We're only playing a game."

But Prahlad knew otherwise. The moment the fire was lit, Prahlad started praying to Lord Vishnu.

King Hiranyakashipu and Holika had forgotten one important detail. Holika's special powers would save her only if she entered the fire alone. This time she had Prahlad with her in the fire. So her magical power did not work and she perished in the flames.

As so many times before, Lord Vishnu came to Prahlad's rescue. The child remained unharmed.

The story of Prahlad teaches that God watches over his followers and that good always wins over evil.

Holika held Prahlad in her lap as they sat in the middle of the raging bonfire.

The Birth of Krishna

Long ago, the kingdom of Mathura in ancient India was ruled by an evil and unpopular king called Kamsa. Years before, he had thrown his father into prison and seized the throne for himself.

King Kamsa had a beautiful sister called Devaki. She was as kind and good as her brother was cruel. She married a handsome prince, called Vasudeva, who came to live at Kamsa's court.

One day, King Kamsa heard a voice coming from the sky.

"Be careful, O King!" the voice warned. "Your sister's eighth child will kill you."

Hearing this, King Kamsa was furious. He was also very frightened. Immediately, he threw Devaki and Vasudeva into prison, and had them guarded, day and night.

Many years went by. Devaki and Vasudeva had seven children. And each time a baby was born, King Kamsa took it away and had it killed.

King Kamsa threw Vasudeva and Devaki into prison on hearing the warning from the sky.

Meanwhile, Lord Vishnu heard of Kamsa's wickedness and decided to act.

"I shall be born as Devaki's eighth child," Vishnu said, "and put an end to King Kamsa for good."

So, one midnight in August, the prison was filled with a dazzling light, and Krishna was born.

"He's so beautiful," sobbed Devaki. "I wish we could save his life."

Then Vasudeva heard a voice.

"Take the baby and cross the river," it said. "The gods will make sure that you are safe."

The gods made sure the doors opened silently and the guards slept peacefully. Vasudeva picked up the baby Krishna and crept out of the prison.

It had been raining hard for many days and a fierce wind had whipped the river into a raging torrent.

▲ In **mandirs**, images of Krishna (left) are often accompanied by those of his companion, Radha (right).

Lord Krishna

Krishna is one of the most popular and widely worshipped Hindu gods. In pictures and images, Krishna is shown playing the flute to call the milkmaids to play. He is also the hero of the **Bhagavad Gita**, one of the most sacred Hindu texts.

▲ Children are often dressed up as Krishna to celebrate the god's birthday.

Birthday Celebrations

In August or September, Hindus celebrate Krishna's birthday with the festival of Janmashtami. In temples dedicated to Krishna, an image of the baby Krishna is placed in a cradle. People also sing songs praising Krishna and act out the story of his birth.

When Vasudeva reached the riverbank, the wind dropped and the water became calm and still. The gods sent a huge, many-headed serpent to protect baby Krishna from the storm. Vasudeva lifted Krishna above his head and waded across the river.

Vasudeva finally reached the village of Vrindavan. He made his way to the home of a cowherd, Nanda, and his wife, Yashoda. They had just had a baby girl. Vasudeva crept into the house and laid Krishna in place of the baby girl. Then he hurried back to the prison with the baby girl and told Devaki that their son was safe.

Next day, King Kamsa rushed in and snatched the baby from Devaki. When Kamsa tried to kill it, it flew into the air. The baby was really a goddess.

"The child you look for is safe," she warned, "and will kill you one day."

The king was furious at being tricked.

"I'll find the boy and kill him," he screamed, "if it's the last thing I do."

But all his efforts to locate and kill Krishna failed.

Years later, a wise man told King Kamsa that Krishna was still alive and well. The king decided on a cunning plan. He invited Krishna to the palace to take part in a wrestling contest.

"I'll send the giants, Mustik and Chaur, to fight him," he said. "He'll be no match for them."

But Krishna killed the giants before they could do him any harm. And then he killed wicked King Kamsa, just as the voice from the sky had foretold.

The gods sent a many-headed serpent to protect Vasudeva and baby Krishna from the storm.

Ganesh and His Elephant Head

High on Mount Kailasha in the mighty Himalayas lived Lord Shiva and his wife, Parvati. Lord Shiva was one of the great gods of the universe and was often away from home. As Parvati waited for him, she felt lonely and bored.

One day she had an idea.

"I'll make myself a baby," she thought, "to keep me company."

Parvati found some earth and water, and mixed them together to make soft clay. She shaped the clay into arms, legs, head

Parvati was lonely. So she made a boy out of clay to keep her company.

and a round tummy to make a baby boy. Then she put him in the sun to dry. Soon he opened his eyes and smiled at her. Parvati was overjoyed.

Parvati named her son Ganesh, and from that day on, they were never apart. They went everywhere together. Even though Shiva had still not returned, Parvati was not lonely or bored anymore.

One sunny day, Parvati and Ganesh went for a long walk in the mountains. It was hot, and soon Parvati was tired. She noticed a refreshing pool of water and wanted to stop and bathe in it.

"Can you keep guard while I'm bathing?" she asked Ganesh. "And make sure that you don't let anyone come near the pool?"

Ganesh was happy to do as Parvati wished. He sat down on a rock while his mother stepped into the cool water.

Some time later, Ganesh saw a figure coming up the mountain path. It was Shiva returning home.

▲ People place images of Ganesh over doorways to invite good luck into their houses.

Worshipping Ganesh

One of the best-loved Hindu **deities**, Ganesh is the god of wisdom and good fortune. Hindus pray to Ganesh whenever they start a new or important task, such as going on a journey or moving house. They believe that he can remove all obstacles. Because of this, his image is seen everywhere.

Ganesh's Birthday

The festival of Ganesh Chaturthi celebrates Ganesh's birthday in August or September. In Mumbai, India, people parade huge images of Ganesh through the streets, accompanied by lots of music and dancing. At the end of the festivities, the people drop the images into the sea.

▼ People drop images of Ganesh into rivers and seas towards the end of Ganesh Chaturthi.

Shiva had heard the sound of splashing coming from the pool and realised that it must be Parvati. He longed to see her and began walking towards the water, only to find a strange little boy blocking his way.

"Stop right there!" the boy ordered.

Shiva was astonished. He was not used to taking orders from anyone.

"Let me go past," he said, angrily, "or you will be sorry."

"I will not," the boy replied, standing firm.

This put Shiva into a terrible temper. He pulled out his sword and cut the boy's head off.

Parvati rushed to see what was happening. She screamed when she saw Ganesh lying on the ground.

"Look what you've done!" she cried. "You've killed our beautiful son!"

"But we haven't got a son," said Shiva, confused. "So how could I have killed him?"

"I made him out of clay," sobbed Parvati. "To keep me company."

Shiva promised to do anything she wanted to make things better.

"Then bring him back to life," she said.

Sword in hand, Shiva set off for the forest to find a new head for Ganesh. The first animal he saw was an elephant. Shiva cut off its great head and took it home. He fitted it on to the boy's body, and then breathed on him to bring him back to life. Parvati was thrilled to get her son back. From that day on this elephant-headed god has always been associated with good luck.

Shiva placed an elephant's head on to the boy's body and brought him back to life.

25

Lakshmi and the Sea of Milk

Once, long ago, a holy man called Durvasa had a **garland** of flowers that never wilted. He gave the flowers to Lord Indra, the king of the gods. In turn, Indra gave the flowers to his favourite elephant, who trampled them into the ground.

Durvasa was furious. He cursed Indra and all the other gods and warned that they would lose their power because it had made them proud and vain. Their power gone, the gods were defeated by the demons and thrown out of Heaven.

The gods went to see Lord Brahma, the creator of the universe, to ask him for his help.

At that time, before the world began, the sea was made of milk. Many precious treasures were hidden in the sea, including a magical liquid called **amrita**.

"The sea of milk must be **churned**," Lord Brahma told the gods, "to get the amrita out. If you drink the amrita, you will live for ever."

But the gods could not do such a difficult job alone. They agreed to work with the demons, just this once.

The gods and demons worked together to churn the sea of milk so they could get the amrita.

Together, the gods and the demons pulled up the huge mountain, Mount Mandara, and put it in the sea. They then wound Vasuki, the huge king of snakes, around the mountain.

The gods held the tail of the snake. The demons held the head. Then they began to pull the snake to and fro, faster and faster, until the sea started to froth and foam. Soon, the mountain was spinning so fast that it threatened to break the Earth to pieces. So the gods sent a huge tortoise for the mountain to stand on.

Creation Stories

The churning story is part of the Hindu creation story. The story goes that, long ago, there was nothing on earth except a white lotus flower floating in the sea of milk. Inside the flower, Lord Brahma, the creator of the universe, was fast asleep. When he woke up, he began the task of creating the world.

▼ This is a **mandir** in Pushkar, India where people can pray to Lord Brahma, the creator of the universe.

▲ The goddess Lakshmi is usually shown wearing fine clothes and lots of gold jewellery.

Lakshmi

Lakshmi is the goddess of beauty, wealth and luck. Images of Lakshmi show her with four arms, each representing one of her powers. She holds lotus flowers, which are symbols of purity and spiritual power. As the goddess of wealth, Lakshmi is worshipped by some Hindus at Diwali, when they celebrate the beginning of the business year.

Soon many wonderful treasures began to appear from the sea. There was a heavenly tree, which made wishes come true, and a flying elephant which Lord Indra took to ride on. There was a cow, which was given to the gods, and the moon, which Lord Shiva took to wear on his head. And, of course, there was a golden **goblet** of amrita, the greatest treasure of all.

As soon as the amrita came out of the sea, Lord Vishnu came down from nearby Mount Meru and snatched the goblet away. He did not want the demons to drink the liquid and become more evil than they already were.

Then an amazing sight appeared. A beautiful goddess rose from the waves in the middle of the milky sea. Her name was Lakshmi. She was standing on a lotus flower and holding

another lotus in her hand. The god of the sea gave her fabulous clothes and jewellery, and put a garland of lotus flowers into her hands.

While the gods and demons watched in surprise, Lakshmi went up to Lord Vishnu and put the garland around his neck. Then she became Lord Vishnu's wife. Vishnu carried Lakshmi from the ocean to his home on Mount Meru. From then on, each time Vishnu descended to the Earth in any form, he was always accompanied by Lakshmi as his wife.

The goddess Lakshmi rose from the sea of milk on a lotus flower.

Glossary

amrita – the liquid that gives power and life

avatar – the form in which the god Vishnu is born on Earth

Bhagavad Gita – one of the sacred texts of Hinduism in which Lord Krishna gives people guidelines on how they should live their lives

Brahman – an invisible force beyond the world in which we live

churn – shake or agitate with a continuous to and fro motion

coronation – ceremony to crown someone as a king

deity – god or goddess

diya – oil lamp made of clay

garland – necklace of flowers

goblet – drinking glass with a base and stem

kiln – furnace or oven for burning, baking, or drying clay pots and bricks

mandir – Hindu temple

moksha – freedom from the mortal world of ordinary experience

Ramayana – a Hindu sacred text that relates the story of the god Rama

sanatana dharma – a phrase that means "eternal teaching". It is what Hindus call their beliefs.

Find Out More

Websites

http://www.sln.org.uk/storyboard/l3.htm

This page lists stories with a Hindu theme.

http://www.reonline.org.uk/allre/tt_nframe.php?http://www.
hindukids.org/stories/

A site that recounts several popular stories from Hinduism.

http://www.reonline.org.uk/allre/tt_nframe.php?http://atschool.
eduweb.co.uk/manorlh/hinduism/hindui.html

A site written for children between the ages of seven and eleven.

Books

*Mythological Stories for Children and Adults: Hindu Tales from the
Sanskrit* by Arthur Bell and S. M. Mitra
Publisher: Arc Manor, 2008

QED Stories from Faiths: Krishna Steals the Butter and Other Stories by
Anita Ganeri
Publisher: QED Publishing, 2007

Stories from Bhagavatham by Gouri V. Suresh
Publisher: Bharatiya Vidya Bhavan, 2004

Index